An Operating Model for Business Agility

This edition published as part of the series
Agile for Managers

2nd edition
© 2022 Russ Lewis All rights reserved
ISBN: 9798391416739
Cover design: Canva Magic Design (artificial intelligence)

Updates available via www.agile-for-managers.com.
Contact the author via www.russlewis.com or say
hello@russlewis.com.

With Thanks

Everything you read in this short book is the result of many years' collaboration and co-creation with managers, agilists, and colleagues. I recall discussions back in 2016 with my dear friends Manoj Ramchandani and Andrea Darabos, without whose on-going support and wisdom we would have nothing more than ideas on a napkin. Luca Willington, Lynsey Mahmood, Rod Willis, and Pam Ashby who helped me prepare a submission for the Harvard Business Review. Raymond Hoffman, Evan Leybourn, Ashleigh Ducker, and Mike Burrows who gave me actionable feedback as I struggled to communicate the concepts. Andy Farmer, whose unique perspective on readership has changed the way I write. Ilse and Bram, whose peer-reviewing of the first release was delivered at speed and with laser focus.

Ethical considerations prevent me from mentioning managers by name, you know who you are, and know how grateful I am to you. As well as helping me develop the concepts, each of you has helped me improve my thinking and writing, and this is what I want to publicly thank you for.

Thank you, all of you.

Contents

About the author

Russ Lewis is a coach, mentor, and recognised agile specialist who helps executives, managers, and teams improve their organisations. He designed and led successful transformations in organisations of two hundred to two hundred-thousand employees. His business agility leadership development program was so popular and inclusive at HSBC, that senior leaders were prepared to join a year-long waiting list just to participate.

An early adopter of Agile methods and service-based architectures, Russ led the team that designed and built the contactless fares system that millions of passengers use every day in London. His software has supported functions within Best Western Hotels, British Telecom, Toyota, and the Metropolitan police. His one-week kick-start for agile development assured the success of scores of teams. He rescued countless IT projects and improvement programmes, and taught thousands of attendees as an author and instructor for Learning Tree International.

For his practitioner doctorate, Russ investigated the shift in the role of managers - away from handing-down decisions or administering policies. That job was important when the operating model was based on delivering a 5-year strategy, as resources really needed careful management and skillful optimisation. To navigate the complexity and plurality of the digital age, managers are increasingly reliant on soft skills. Leading collaborations and clarifying priorities with stakeholders, digital age managers learn alongside the people who report to them as fellow knowledge workers. This theory explains the ways managers create the conditions for success, developing the firms' capabilities whilst managing its tensions.

Russ lives in Oxfordshire with his wife, daughter, son, a dog, and a cat.

Introduction

The manager's world has changed. Middle managers considered "frozen" are blamed for everything wrong with work. Instead of getting recognition for magically keeping everything going, they are allegedly responsible for preventing change and maintaining bureaucracy. Their hours are ridiculously long because there is an ever-increasing amount of administration to get through and an ever-decreasing number of people to do it. If there was a better job to go to, they may take it, but most sectors have similar management and operating models.

Those high-enough up in the hierarchy to be styled as "leaders" are experiencing unprecedented transparency and uncertainty. The size of a large organisation generates so many upwards-facing priorities that it has to operate by downward delegation and upward reporting. Yet the hard work, expertise, and quick decision-making that brought them to the top seem to have lost the long-term impact they once had. What used to be a complicated business that "ran by the numbers," has become a complex web of forces and it feels like there is nothing solid to stand-on anymore. The best options are staying for the long haul by keeping one's head down, or making a big impact fast, to get to the next position.

Agile for Managers considers this situation from the perspective of all managers (top, middle, bottom, or whatever). It asks:

How can we make better decisions right now?

How can established firms transition to the digital age?

What is happening to organisations and why?

This book series is a practical guide for smart managers, who want to know how to increase *business agility* to improve operational effectiveness. I provide the tools and techniques, and trust readers to apply their resourcefulness and expertise to work-out how to use them. Each book in the series is intended to be a very quick read. This one provides just-enough "big picture" information to inspire the most transformational readers to set a direction and start leading improvements.

This book is organised like this:

> *Chapter 1. Running and changing the business;* the lens described in chapter 1 reveals crucial new information. That gives you the power to match each situation with the appropriate control mechanism, making your responsibilities easier to manage, and more likely to succeed.

> *Chapter 2. Making investment decisions that increase profits;* factoring the "cost of delay" into decision-making will help you balance the need to reduce costs, with the financial implications of that view. It is super-easy to do this when you know which data to compare.

> *Chapter 3. Decision-making as an improvable process;* experience and "gut instinct" still feature in the digital age, just not as much as they have in the past. Systematising decisions, as described here, will increase the speed and quality of the services you deliver, and help you manage its continual improvement.

Chapter 4. Preventing inexcusable wastes; feedback mechanisms are easy to build and simple to operate. It is a wonder they are so often overlooked or misunderstood as they are guaranteed to protect your sources of profit, both existing and exploratory.

Chapter 5. Amplifying customer value; there is more to an organisation than can be seen or measured. Since managers shape the work context, they are ideally positioned to amplify the capabilities needed to increase the flow of value to customers in the digital age.

Chapter 6. Not your grandfather's workplace; investigates the emerging role of the manager as leader of business agility improvement. I propose three ways managers can transform their organisations today.

This first book in the series presents the big picture, in the form of a better model of the organisation. Subsequent books consider how each part of that model can be used to engage stakeholders.

The second book looks at improving prioritisation and decision-making. Diving deeply into something taken for granted, it is a thought-provoking examination of the decision-making systems needed to run an effective business operation. I describe how prioritising demand creates clarity and alignment throughout the business, how to set measurable outcomes, how to match demand to capacity, and how to connect strategy with execution.

The third book sets-out the way managers can achieve predictable and agile delivery in their departments and business units. Notice how everything comes together within the delivery systems of an organisation but that business effectiveness is the result of collaboration and high-quality decision-making at all levels of the organisation. It covers topics that are broadly familiar to Lean and Agile practitioners, however my approach combines leadership, management, and delivery as "jobs to be done," rather than separate roles. It describes measurable business agility; the desired outcome of most agile or digital transformations.

Book four's focus is on the hidden tensions that tend to slow-down established organisations with conflicting priorities, bureaucracy, and inertia. I explain the sources of these tensions by drawing on emerging research that identifies six basic tensions that exist in all organisations. Then I describe the methods that have been shown to be effective in helping managers resolve the tensions. Many of these are soft skills methods, appropriate for tensions in complex situations with many stakeholders and no simple solutions.

The series as a whole describes a methodology of organisational transformation. It is the transformation of management, by managers. I cannot think of anyone better qualified to do that job, can you?

1 Running and changing the Business

This chapter helps you increase agility by matching predictable and emergent activities with the appropriate controls.

Predictable and emergent Characteristics

The lens of predictability and emergence is powerful because it reveals the challenges hidden within each situation. With this information, your expertise and wisdom will guide you to make the right decisions.

We use different operating systems for planning and for doing. Where planning is rational, based on prediction and assumption, doing is intuitive. We respond to emergent patterns in the moment. The *predictable* system is complicated, like a mechanical watch. Each watch is built to a predetermined technical specification based on well-known and reliable principles, then behaves exactly as its designer expects. The *emergent* system is complex, and highly unpredictable. "Ah-ha" insights and game-changing discoveries come unexpectedly. Such as:

> When Alexander Fleming returned from his holidays, he noticed something strange in a petri dish in his laboratory, and then isolated a mould able to kill bacteria. Fleming was a bacteriologist, so it was *likely* that his work would contribute to that field of knowledge. But Fleming's discovery occurred in 1928, fourteen years before the first

patient was treated with penicillin. Penicillin *emerged* from Fleming's discovery over time.[1]

What, when, and how emergent work delivers value, is only known after it has happened. Whereas, obtaining predictable value is often the result of planning and coordinating resources. Industrial age wealth was mostly created by organising, market research, product design, technical design, marketing, manufacture, and distribution resources. Of course, the competence to predict, plan, and control organisations is another resource. Emergent value, such as converting a naturally occurring bacterium into life-saving penicillin, depends on the situation and the prevailing conditions. Nobody could predict who would read about Fleming's discovery; how curious they were to follow-up; what else was known at the time; what funding would become available; or who else would get involved.

Balancing run and change Activities

Most managers are familiar with the difference between "run" and "change." This lens differentiates activities that mainly produce predictable, or emergent value. Activities that deliver predictable value allow "Operations" to "run the business." But as external conditions change, so do the markets that supply money to that business, both as consumers of its services and financers of its ambitions. Therefore, businesses must also innovate, and "change the business" to stimulate financial growth and respond to changes in their market. Even non-commercial organisations must adapt to the evolving needs of the society they serve. Organisational "ambidexterity" is therefore desirable, if not essential.

The challenge is balancing both forces at the same time by recognising the overlaps and tensions between them. Most large, existing organisations solve this problem structurally, separating run and change into different departments. We may dislike some consequences of "silos," but they enable operations functions to optimise for predictable value activities, leaving research and development departments free to work on emergent value activities.

These characteristics are summarised in Table 1 below:

	Emergent value activities	Predictable value activities
Characteristics	Solutions emerge over time, or not.	Solutions and necessary resources are predetermined.
	Being effective is more important than being efficient.	Efficiency is necessary to maintain profits and competitiveness.
Forces	Mostly changing the business	Mostly running the business
Challenge	Balancing forces and tensions	

Table 1 Characteristics of predictable and emergent value activities

Agile control mechanisms match emergent value Activities

Imagine you are funding an emergent value activity, such as the development of a new smart billing and contactless fares system. You would want to know if your investment is going to pay-off and how much over-budget it is going to be. According to Shashi Verma, who was in this situation in 2012, once the work has begun, the next key decision is to "decide if you can trust your team to deliver."[2]

The team published a list of the outstanding outcomes and provided regular updates on progress. In June it looked like Table 2 below:

Month	Planned goal	What actually happened
Mar	Build prototype engine to construct simple journeys only	Processed 1m journeys in 6 minutes in memory but took 2 hours when written to the database.
Apr	Support multi-stage journeys (like a sat-nav in reverse)	Threw-away code and rebuilt as state engine, storing only state changes.
May	Provide user interface and user-friendly testing language	Not in the original plan, but people were getting curious and keen to see if the engine could reconstruct their journeys to work.
Jun	Add logic for all fifty journey types	
Jul	Build journey pricing service	
Aug	Support pre-purchased tickets and daily charge capping	
Sept	User and admin interfaces	
Oct	Soft launch & investigate weekly charge capping	
Nov	Wider launch and user interface refinement	
Dec	Documentation	

Table 2 Agile delivery plan

The list is both a record of progress and a plan. That is appropriate because it is still emerging. Other points worth noticing are:

The team delivered consistently according to its predictions for previous months. The most-difficult challenges were prioritised, leaving easier (less risky) work for later.

Change was welcomed. In May, someone had the insight to open-up testing to stakeholders.

Agile practices ensured the cost and mission remained fixed throughout, allowing stakeholders to both control the work, and adapt to opportunities and obstacles.

That was an example of how agile practices provide simple and effective controls for emergent value activities. The outcome provides the direction, but the way to reach it, and what the solution is, remains unknown until the solution is up and running. In this case, work was completed on-time and to budget. It enabled Transport for London to deliver a contactless fares capability to London's buses, then to the entire public transport network.[3]

Of course, there are many parts to any project. The predictable parts can be managed using plan-driven controls, but specific areas of uncertainty may benefit from agile controls. I introduced the distinction so that we can be aware of it in the real-world. To support that aim, let us compare controlling emergent and predictable value activities.

Comparing control Mechanisms

When the activity's output is known, the solution and most of the problems encountered whilst getting there, are predictable. Much of what we do has a predetermined solution. Provisioning a new data centre, migrating to the next version of Windows, moving to, or building a new house are best managed by predicting, planning, and controlling resources and activities. I do not doubt readers are familiar with "plan-driven" controls since traditional project management methods are strongly plan-driven.

Adding financial controls to the comparison, reveals how feedback helps decision-making by signalling when to stop, reduce, or increase the funding of the activity. This works because the funding controls the capacity, and capacity controls output. See Table 3 below:

	Emergent value activities	Predictable value activities
Control mechanisms	"Inspect and adapt" provides adaptive *outcome*-based control.	"Plan-driven" control compares *output* to predetermined plans.
	Daily inspection of progress made progress towards desired outcome and weekly adaptation of the methods used.	Performance indicators send signals for managers to interpret (eg. throughput over time, number of defects).
Financial control	Stop funding when nothing of value has emerged for three months. Confirmed by "go and see."	Stop funding when production is no longer profitable. Provided by feedback loops (eg. matching supply to actual demand).

Table 3 Controls of predictable and emergent value activities

Predictable value activities produce measurable revenues or satisfy actual customer orders. There are no similar mechanisms for emergent activities other than being physically present and using one's senses to decide if the activity is valuable or not. It is for situations like these that quality improvement and management guru W Edwards Deming, who was actually a statistician, warned managers:

"One cannot be successful on visible figures alone."

W Edwards Deming [4]

Smart readers will be ahead of me, realising that once a solution has emerged, it starts to move towards predictability. This movement is one reason that balancing these activities is so difficult. Whilst *efficiency* applies to producing predictable value, it is *effectiveness* that matters when developing solutions. And both activities benefit from continuous improvement.

Improving the Activities

When it comes to improvement, managers must make another important distinction. Predictable value activities can be made more efficient because the output has been predetermined, whereas emergent value activities become more effective at producing an outcome.

To select the right improvement approach, we need to recognise how value is added in each activity type.

Adding predictable Value

Although we know everyone makes a unique contribution at work, and customer value matters above all other considerations, improvements are often made on the assumption that *workers* need to become more productive. This is partially true for predictable value activities, where resources can be replaced by faster or cheaper versions. Machines and facilities, as well as managers and workers, are candidates for this method of improvement. Moral concerns notwithstanding, it can leave people feeling like they are valued as though nothing more than a cog in the machine.

Machines, and the corresponding "machine model" mentality, have changed over time, but slowly. To put that rate of change into perspective, and based on my understanding of events:

> Adam Smith's "division of labour" has been improving the efficiency of complicated and predictable work ever since his publication in 1776 of transforming pin manufacturing (measured by productivity).

> Henry Ford improved efficiency (measured by time) of mass production by removing as much variation as possible from the
> Model T's production processes.

> After WW2, as Japan was rebuilding its economy, Taiichi Ohno developed "Just In Time" production to improve efficiency (measured by waste reduction) at Toyota.

These pioneers built-on previously established knowledge and improved already-established production methods. Their improvements are seen as transformational now because we know that they work, and why. But it took time and evidence for most manufacturers to adopt their innovations.

Adding emergent Value

Various customer-centric approaches were developed in the 1990s and these, combined with emerging design philosophies, created the conditions for the technology transformation we now experience. Agile, as a term, was chosen by software developers. In 2001, it represented "better ways of developing software" than the prevailing approaches.

Software solutions emerge as the result of collaborative design and experimentation, not the production of a predetermined design. Hence, the authors of the Agile Manifesto for Software Development showed how the complex and emergent work of solving a poorly defined set of problems is more effective when the development team collaborates both with the problem-owners, and each other.

Emergent value depends on people interacting with technology, collaboratively. The social aspect of this work is as important as the technical, but impossible for us to define precisely at the moment.

Although managers are sometimes uncomfortable when "soft skills" enter the workplace, psychological factors are bound to affect performance when people use brainpower to create value. Managers create the conditions of work by the ways they behave, actions they take and the language they use. Therefore, managers can improve the effectiveness of emergent value activities by creating the micro conditions needed to understand complex situations and find-out what happens as they try to address them. Appropriate tactics include:

Acting more like a coach than a controller.

Focussing on collaboration, clarity, and learning.

Building trust and increasing autonomy.

> Actively listening to people without presuming to solve their problems.

We saw how trust and autonomy were critical for developing TfL's contactless fares system. Google's research into managing showed that their best managers use coaching techniques[5] and their most effective teams; feel safe, feel like they can depend on each other, have clear goals, know their purpose, and believe their work has impact.[6]

Perhaps the biggest impact on effectiveness comes from handing-over the control of the methods of doing work, to the people who are doing that work. The reason is simple, the restrictions of one-size-fits-all processes makes predictable work more efficient, but the effectiveness of emergent value work depends on the variety provided by its participants.

> *"Agile development focuses on the talents and skills of individuals and molds process to specific people and teams, not the other way around."*
> Alistair Cockburn & Jim Highsmith[7]

Recognising the difference between predictable and emergent value activity situations tells managers which control mechanisms and strategies are appropriate. This is summarised in the comparison Table 4 below:

	Emergent value activities	Predictable value activities
Value added by	"Soft skills" that create optimum conditions (eg. trust, diversity, openness, autonomy).	Improving the process and reducing variation to increase throughput (eg. towards mass-production).
	Noticing patterns and intervening when anti-patterns are recognised.	Reducing costs by outsourcing and resource optimisation.
Process control	People-first.	Process-first.
Improvement strategy	People create, control, and improve their own processes.	Processes designed and optimised by experts.
	Encourage variety of output, reduce variation within each process.	Limit variety of output, and eliminate variation in all processes.
Growth strategy	Produce greater variety of products and services.	Produce as much as possible of the same.

Table 4 Value and improvement characteristics of predictable and emergent value activities

Summarising the Situation

The situation has changed from when we set out together, so I suggest we pause for a moment to review. Military strategists recognise the value of "situational awareness," and it is common sense, yet we can be so busy we forget to reflect. Cults protect themselves from common sense by making sure any new information is rejected or ridiculed before it can change member's beliefs. We are smarter than that.

The need for organisations to balance both "run" and "change" the business, was our first consideration. Separating these activities structurally was effective in the machine age, when an investment decision resulted in separate design, build, and operate activities. Operations looked-after making profits, and it did not matter if design and build were separate silos or even different companies, since the output of each stage predicted the value produced by the next. Dividing work by function improved efficiency, as the pioneers of mass production showed.

In the digital age, more of what customers value is developed collaboratively. Value emerges through understanding customer behaviour, experimenting with technology, and collaborating to create new solutions. Variety is valuable in this context. People doing the work develop and improve their processes as part of their work. Such self-organising behaviour characterises agile practices and increases business agility.

Agile methods are most appropriate for complex situations such as emergent value-creating activities. Predict, plan, and control, or plan-driven methods suit complicated, repetitive activities. Efficiency of these activities can be increased by reducing both the variety of the output, and variation of the processes that produces it (mass production). Henry Ford's goal was to produce cars more quickly than anyone else, so he chose a single colour for all cars and parts. Black was probably cheaper and more reliable than other colours.[8]

The predictable and emergent lens helps us appreciate these differences and make decisions that are more appropriate when controlling and improving activities at work.

Practical Application

Thinking about the activities within your business unit, which produce mostly emergent value, and which are more predictable?

Where do they overlap?

What emergent value steps do you notice within predictable value activities?

2 Making investment decisions that increase Profits

This chapter helps you make more-profitable decisions by factoring the "costs of delay" into decision-making.

High-stakes investment decisions

Predictable value activities were the focus of the machine age. Wealth was created by mass-production that followed development and innovation. One barrier to unlimited wealth-creation was developing the capabilities of mass-production at scale and to a quality standard. Think about the traditional music industry, which made and sold copies of the music created by artists. Or the motor industry in its heyday, which mass-produced and mass-marketed a few thousand designs into more than one billion cars.[i]

A legacy of that thinking is that a new product has two distinct phases, explore and exploit.

> The first is a capital investment phase during which the necessary resources, such as premises, machines, and skills, are acquired, *exploring* possibilities, and *expanding* the organisation's capabilities.

---

[i] One billion cars had been produced by 2010, according to https://www.worldometers.info/cars/.

The second is an operational phase, during which the capability is *optimised* and *exploited* for as long as possible.

The decision-making stakes are high in the first phase, because the second phase depends on its outcome. In this sense, investment decisions are strategic. As such, they need to withstand shareholder scrutiny, be properly informed, and methodically made. This is not always the case.

In manufacturing, which is our next example, the first phase has a pre-defined and predictable outcome but with identifiable uncertainty. As we are about to see, the cost of delaying production may be more important than price when acquiring machinery yet is frequently overlooked.

Factoring cost of delay into decision-making

One of my favourite metaphors, probably because it is absurdly out of place in high-tech situations, is a machine that makes sausages. Imagine this scenario:

> Our sausages are so successful, we have decided to increase profits by scaling-up production and will invest in a new sausage-making facility downtown. The planned processing facility has predictable value. Its capacity (packs per hour) and profitability (revenue after operational costs) are predictable and have been factored into the design and requests for tender. Procurement has produced a shortlist of four suppliers that meet our criteria.

> Their quotes to build the plant are $5m, $5.5m,
> $6m, and $7.5m.

Having spent a lot of time and money arriving at a shortlist, making the wrong decision at this point is the worst possible outcome. So how do you decide which bid to accept?

If your purchasing policy, or decision, is to select based on price, you have a 25% chance of making the right decision (any one of four suppliers could be the best). If you make the decision based on the supplier's history of completion versus estimate, you can make the right decision with confidence. Of course, this is not to say you will prevent catastrophe befalling the project, only that you can select the best of the four candidate suppliers. Here is why:

> If you make $1 profit per pack, and the plant
> processes 10,000 packs per hour, the new plant is
> capable of yielding $10,000k per day. Four
> month's delay in opening and operating that plant
> will have cost $1.2m in lost profit. Again, that is
> profit, not revenue or cost savings.

Comparing suppliers by price *and* the reliability of their estimates provides decision-makers with the minimum information they need to make a selection. This is true because we were making decisions for a predictable value activity and were able to factor the explicit costs of delay into the equation to account for that uncertainty.

Historical data about the accuracy of the suppliers' predictions was an appropriate variable, after price, on which to base a decision.[ii]

Estimating opportunity Cost

For "product development" companies, such as pharmaceutical and publishing, the first phase has significantly more complex characteristics. The cost of delay cannot be calculated because an immeasurable number of variables makes prediction impossible. For instance:

> The decision to develop a drug to help manage coronary conditions led to the discovery that it was more effective for the treatment of erectile dysfunction (Sildenafil, better known as Viagra).
>
> Twelve publishers made the decision to decline J K Rowling's opportunity to publish her "Harry Potter" novel.[9]

In such complex situations, there are no right or wrong decisions. The opposite of a good decision may be a slightly better decision. There are too many opportunities and not enough capacity or time to wait for the best result to emerge. To put this in context:

─────────────────────────

[ii] This example of cost of delay was adapted from a lecture by Eli Goldratt.

Looking-back in time at publishers rejecting Harry Potter, makes for a good story because those twelve publishers missed the opportunity of a lifetime. But it was one out of how many thousands of opportunities? Of the few hundred books they did decide to publish, were enough sold that the firms increased their profits? With that information, did they make reasonable decisions with the opportunities presented at the time?

Product development in the sausage-making world is also context sensitive. Deciding what the next sausage ingredient should be, or which market sector to aim at, are essentially "bets" on the market. There are unlimited ingredients and sectors to choose from, some of which will be more successful than others. Whichever permutation is selected, incurs the "opportunity costs" of missing-out on all the others.

Unlike the cost of delay example, which we were able to predict and calculate, opportunity costs can be "guesstimated" using relative estimation and "group wisdom."[iii]

Try this experiment with people at work:

[iii] In 1907 Galton showed a crowd of people could make surprisingly accurate guesses after watching a crowd of people guess the weight of an ox.

Ask people to estimate worker disengagement, relative to one person feeling disengaged one day per month as a "1" (relative estimation).

Without sharing people's answers in advance, you should notice a tendency towards similar estimates. The more people you ask, the closer their results will be to a score for worker disengagement in your organisation (group wisdom).

This is useful because when stakeholders make an estimate, it is based on their informed opinion, an "educated guess." When several estimates are made, it can remove biases such as ego and defending the ideas in which we are invested. Experience-based judgements can easily become contaminated by invisible forces such as these.

We shall return to the problem of making investment decisions for emergent value activities in section two, in the context of prioritising demand. Before that, I thought of adding a little variety to summarising.

A visual Summary

I have another metaphor to offer. It is the organisation as that ancient and wondrous symbol, the chalice. Feel free to choose the design and shape that most appeals to you, be it; cup, goblet, or elegant glass. Mine would be mediaeval, solid, and squat with a short stem supporting a cup containing sweet mead. Yours can hold any contents you like, as long as it moves like a fluid, agilely.

My PowerPoint skills do not live up to my imagination, so we will have to use a diagram of my chalice. The organisation, including its culture, is the chalice. It looks like this, see Figure 1 below:

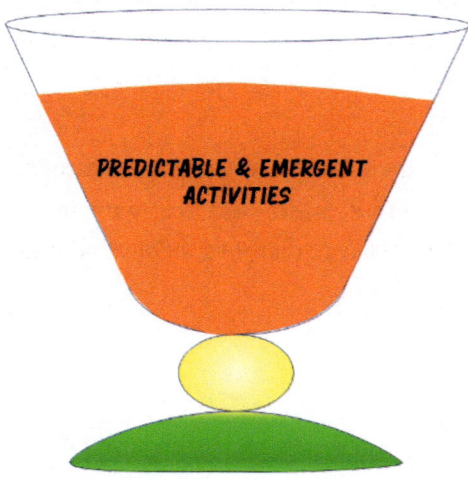

Figure 1 Organisation as a chalice

In chapter 1, we saw how strategy led to the organisation of resources. Those resources, including employees, skills, assets, practices, and tools, are the contents of the cup. We saw that:

Most resources were dedicated to operations (running the business) and focussed on activities that generated predictable value outputs. Their improvement strategy was efficiency, getting as much productivity as possible from the existing resources and solutions.

Other resources were organised into research and development departments, and they explored ways of growing the business by extending the solutions it provided. Their goals were largely outcome-based with solutions that emerged over time.

In this chapter, we considered the organisation in its context within a market. In the next diagram, we can appreciate that the vessel is open-mouthed to allow existing customers to interact with our products and services. And for us to invite potential customers in (to sip the nectar, perhaps?).

Customers are involved with the organisation's deliveries and activities, but are their own, separate organisations. Everyone beyond this chalice's boundary is a stakeholder. See Figure 2 below:

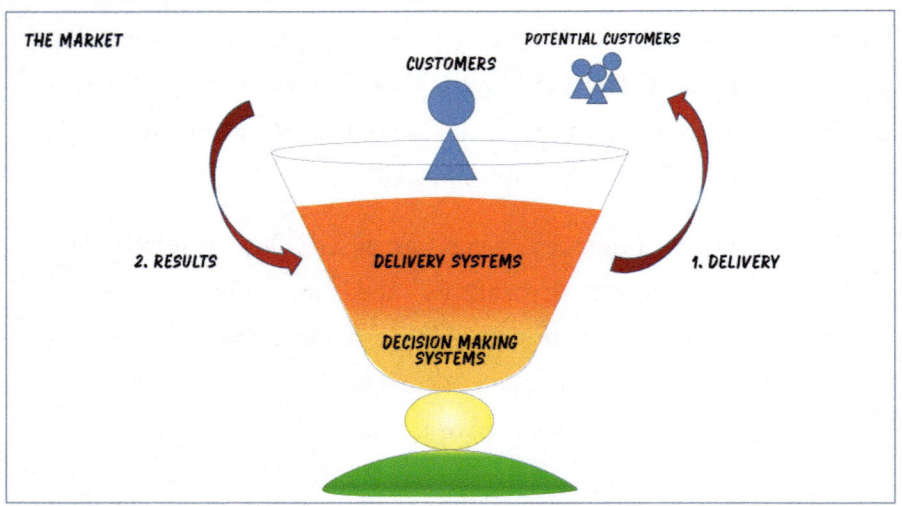

Figure 2 Chalice in context of the market

Creating demand for a product or service means converting potential customers into actual customers. We already had some customers for sausages and now predict the market has the potential for us to create more customers. We decided to deliver more product to the market by building a new facility. Therefore:

> All investment decisions are like "bets" on the market (see arrow 1). Costs can be calculated for predictable value bets and guesstimated for emergent value activities.

> The result of each bet is what matters (see arrow 2). How the boss thinks the market should have responded, or who did what to whom, is irrelevant.

The same reasoning can be applied to on-going (run) and new (change) decisions, which will be a critical feedback loop in chapter 4.

But first, we need to shake things up a bit more. Instead of resources, a word that makes me uncomfortable in reference to people, what if we work with "capabilities?" Instead of dividing the workforce into run and change structures, what if we separated it by "what needs to be done to improve this capability at this moment?" See what you think about it in the next chapter.

Practical Application

What are bets and results in your organisation, and in your business unit? Who are your customers and potential customers, and what value do they expect your organisation and business unit to deliver to them?

3 Decision-making as an improvable Process

This chapter helps you scale and improve decision-making by replacing hierarchical bottlenecks with reliable and improvable decision-making processes.

Capabilities not Resources

Thinking in terms of resources was useful for organising and operationalising strategy, as we did in chapter 1. Once a service is delivering value to its customers, it is better to think in terms of capabilities. Think about paying for your in-store grocery shopping. You just want to be able to pay for the items you are holding right now, whether it is by self-serve, full-serve, or radio-frequency magic. When you are waiting in line, are you thinking "they should open more checkouts" or wondering about "resource optimisation?" Capabilities are better aligned to what is important to customers, than resources.

Figure 3 below shows the sausage-making decision of chapter 2 as an expansion of capabilities:

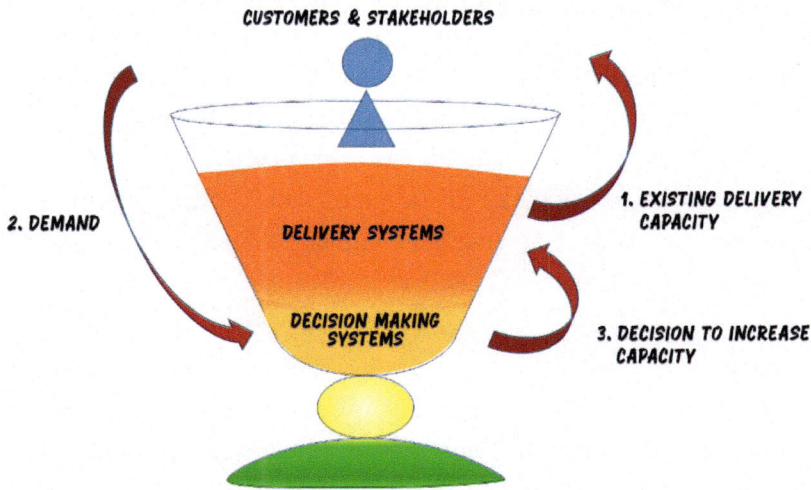

Figure 3 Expanding production capacity as decision-making output

This view shows:

> The results of our original "bet" have paid-off. Our "Delivery Systems" include sausage-making machinery are delivering value to our customers (see arrow1).

> Our belief that we have created more demand than we have current capacity (arrow 2).

> The decision to expand (arrow 3) is the output of a decision-making process. The input to that process being the information above (arrows 1 and 2). This is one of many decision-making processes, hence "Decision-Making Systems."

Separating decision-making from Delivery

The business now has a delivery capability and a decision-making capability. This distinction is not a division of labour, because they are different activities done by the same people. It is a distinction that recognises delivery as a predictable value activity, and decision-making as an emergent activity. It reminds us to use the appropriate methods for each.

Intentionally moving into decision-making, as if it were a dedicated space, is a reminder of the change of operating systems. We now ask, "do we have enough information to make a properly-informed decision?" This deliberate transition allows us to check that all stakeholders are represented and manage any behaviours likely to shut-out inconvenient or challenging information.

"Jobs to be done" by a decision-making Process

Clay Christensen developed the "Jobs to be done" lens, a wonderful way of decoupling problems from solutions, and tasks from job titles.[10]

Everyone makes thousands of micro-choices each day, and most are not worth the effort of systematising. The decisions that are, tend to be context-sensitive and have inputs, outputs, controls, and measures. The main "jobs to be done" by a decision-making system are:

> *Matching the control mechanism to the activity;* selecting plan-driven controls for predictable value activities and agile methods for emergent (discussed in chapter 1).

Prioritising work, clarifying the current priorities of the organisation, and *setting strategic goals and global measures;* to enable local decision-making throughout the organisation (which we will examine in a later book).

Describing the measures that matter for each delivery and *making data-informed decisions;* also featured in later.

These outcomes, and the clear, effective communication of them to everyone, are critical to the organisation. Only if people know the big picture, such as what the organisation values most, can they make decisions locally. If this is not clear, then the pace of work will slow down as people seek hierarchical approval and direction. Similarly, work may halt later, whilst people go back to correct the consequences of assumptions that have been shown to be wrong.

Improving decision-Making

Meetings are often held because a decision is needed. How many of those meetings use the wisdom of stakeholders to convert information into a decision? That is the purpose of a decision-making process. Such meetings are unlikely to go away, but there are ways for you to apply this lens to make them more effective.

Positioning decision-making as a critical capability, allows us to continually improve it, just as any other process. For example:

> During a review of an IT department's decision-making capabilities, managers were asked, "knowing what you know now, how would you have spent last year's budget?"

In general, the steps to improve any process are:

> Clarify the purpose of the process, identify the stakeholders it serves, and how its performance will be measured.

> Make the process visual (and public), so everyone knows how it operates and what is required and delivered at each stage.

> Make one improvement to the process every week, or every time it runs.

Better decision-making improves organisational Performance

Systematising decision-making as a process makes decisions repeatable. Making that process better and better improves organisational performance.

Kent Beck suggests decision-making can be improved by asking:

> Do decisions flow to information?

> Do consequences flow to decisions?

These indicate change in what Kent calls the "social structures" of work.[11] When decisions are made by managers, the flow of work waits until the decision returns to the place it is needed before work can resume. In an agile workplace, managers *create the context* for decisions to be made directly in the flow of work. That depends on the people doing the work being able to step-out of the work and into decision-making, making their decision, then implementing it immediately. Of course, the scope of decision-making, and its consequences, must be agreed in advance. For instance:

> Instead of handing-off operational support, teams that practice "DevOps" take responsibility for developing and operationally supporting the software they build. They perform both development and operations functions. It may take a few support calls before developers find ways to make their systems more resilient, but they do. "Elite" DevOps teams outperform low performers by 300% in terms of failures caused by releasing changes to production but 6500% in terms of time to recover from an incident. They make changes very quickly.[12]

Predictable and Agile Delivery Systems

Sponsors of agile transformation and improvement initiatives usually want a few, very reasonable outcomes. They are:

Delivery of working products in weeks or months.

Reliable estimates of when stakeholders can expect delivery.

The ability to change their minds about what to deliver next.

Whilst the outcomes are better described as "agile delivery" there is no doubt that agile has solutions to the problems implied. Most of the theory comes from the Lean movement, which started in post-war Japan, most famously at Toyota. The problem then, as it remains for managers today, is the control and improvement of "socio-technical systems." The unique combination of people and machines that provides a capability in context. We will examine this further in Section III.

Leaning towards Theory

Lean is a straight-forward approach. Practitioners make decisions based on measurements and can improve running processes because they have the evidence and controls, they need to reduce risk. As much as this appeals to engineers, it fails too, as many managers prefer to follow their instincts and experience. As ever, success lies in combination and is achieved through collaboration.

Part of the fun of Lean is it shows how the most counter-intuitive interventions can prove to be the most effective. For example, slowing down to go faster, reducing the number of activities in progress to increase throughput, and allowing work to be "pulled" through processes, instead of wasting energy pushing it.

"Agilising" a delivery System

If the improvement goal is predictable and agile delivery, the measures that matter could be "lead time" and throughput rate. Lead time is however long it takes for an item to be prioritised as the next piece of work by the decision-making system and its delivery into the hands of its intended users. Throughput is the rate at which individual pieces emerge at the delivery end of a process. In sausage terms:

Lead time is how long a customer waits for an order to be fulfilled.

Throughput is the number of sausages per day that a facility can produce. This measure is usually balanced by defect rate.

If these are our chosen measures of performance, then we must acknowledge they are measures of process performance only. They do not account for any variety of output.

If every sausage we made was a different flavour, and the machine had to be cleaned and reset each time, performance would be lower, but still measurable and improvable.

When we improve the performance of a technical delivery process, our focus is the process, not the output. Improving output is usually a matter of increasing technical competence.

Making an existing delivery system more predictable and more agile is to enter within a delivery process, understand its steps, and sense the opportunities for improvement. In this section we stay outside of the processes, as that is the perspective of top management and one of the perspectives of all managers.

Summarising what just Happened

We split the organisation into two systems. A delivery system, potentially predictable and agile, that represents all the operational capabilities that deliver value to customers, and a decision-making system that represents the decisions that need to be made, including those we have just systematised. Within a department, business area, or team, they would be considered processes, but "system" reminds us that people and tools and time and space are involved, throughout the organisation.

Does it seem reasonable to view an organisation in these terms, so that people can move between delivery and decision work? And do so easily, regardless of their job title or rank in the hierarchy?

Before we put these decision-making processes to use in the next chapters, let us consider the chalice visual again. People within the organisation, the fluid contents of the chalice, move freely between doing their delivery work and taking part in decision-making. Everyone is engaged in improving the organisation's delivery of value to customers, measured by the profit that generates. This is what we see in Figure 4 below:

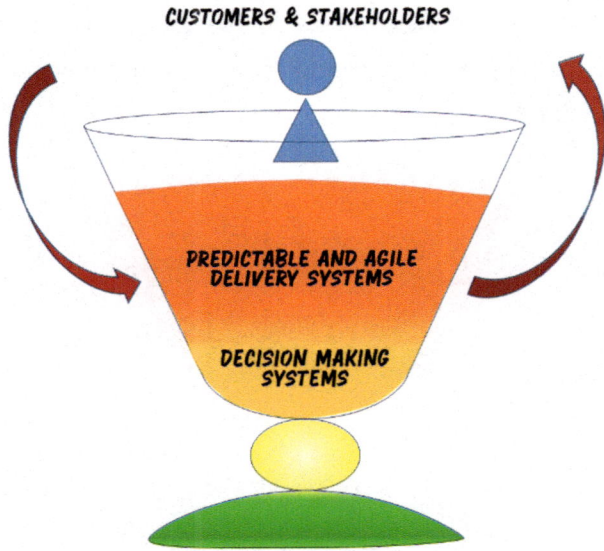

Figure 4 Operating systems in the chalice metaphor

Practical Application

List two or three decisions that affect your team. For each one, try to answer these questions:

Who are the stakeholders and how involved are they in decision-making?

Can you identify a decision-making process. if so, what are its inputs and outputs?

What is the performance evaluation mechanism for this process?

What is being done to improve that performance?

What are the interfaces; how do they inputs arrive and how are the outputs delivered to the teams that rely on those decisions?

4 Preventing inexcusable Wastes

This chapter will help you protect value-generating activities by applying simple feedback mechanisms to prevent avoidable and costly mistakes.

Problems Problems

Managers are disappointed when they realise their organisation keeps making the same mistakes over and again. Too many high-priority initiatives going-on at the same time, too many conflicting priorities, too many projects based on untested assumptions, too many customer complaints, yet there is never enough time to do things right. For example:

> As they got through another annual budget cycle, managers told each other this was the worst it has ever been, agreed to change the process, then got busy catching-up with everything they had put on hold for the previous two months. Predictably, nothing of consequence had changed for many years.

Although it would be a good example of reducing an opportunity cost (see chapter 2), I am not going to tell you how to improve annual budgeting. I shared that story as an example of how much easier it is to continue doing something, than it is to stop or change it. The organisations that do it can afford the wastes it generates. They can afford to wait the ninety days it takes to deliver a technical change. And they can absorb the costs of delay caused by prioritising internal, rather than customer value.

My job in this chapter is to help managers recognise that we can identify wasteful mistakes by observing the systems of work through a different lens, and it is their choice to prioritise their improvement, or not. By choosing to prioritise other activities, managers' action communicates their acceptance of these wastes. That may be a reasonable decision for an overburdened manager determined to avoid seriously complex problems, but it condemns the people within the hierarchy to continue to work amongst them.

Simple Controls

The mechanistic, repetitive behaviour of operational processes means they can be controlled by the simplest of tools, checklists, and feedback loops. When complicated processes are properly controlled, humans can rely on, and re-configure them, to solve complex problems.

Without those controls, wastes are inevitable. The controls are simple, yet they help assure complicated processes. Without these controls, complexity gets into complicated processes, making them unpredictable. Our assumption that complicated processes behave as they should are proved wrong, but we can only know that after the problem has occurred and we look backward to understand why.

Testing Assumptions

As an engineer, I think "go/no-go" gauges are special because they are dedicated to increasing the speed and efficiency of a process. It would be wrong to assume that a letter is the size of a letter, it may be a "Large Letter."

The UK's Royal Mail made the gauge in Figure 5 to check the thickness and width of a letter. Whilst you could use a ruler or a tape measure to compare the sizes of each letter with the permitted dimensions, these slots in a piece of plastic, makes decision-making fast and dependable.

Figure 5 Royal Mail letter-sizing gauge (Image from eBay)

Here are some tests of the assumed effectiveness of communication using feedback mechanisms. Try it on yourself and with others by asking:

How often are you satisfied (or delighted) with the outcome of tasks you delegate?

How many times did you define the criteria for success during delegation, so you would be certain of its completion?

How often did you ask people to explain their understanding of the task back to you, before going away to do it?

How many times did you review the delegation process following delivery or non-delivery of tasks?

My prediction is your answers will be mostly high. If others' are low, they will likely all be low, and you may want to share the following section with them. It embeds feedback mechanisms in places where they are non-negotiable.

Feedback Mechanisms

Processes deliver outputs, so monitoring the value a process is delivering is a crucial control, best implemented as a feedback mechanism. In a sausage-making start-up feedback mechanisms are humans:

Jake: "Why are we still making these pomegranate and walnut sausages? Nobody likes them and those pomegranates take-up a lot of space."

Emma: "Because we have orders. Do you really think I would make them if they weren't selling?"

But what happens when Emma is no longer keeping an eye on the orders and Jake stops asking questions? Maybe others will continue making the same sausages without question because "that's what we've always done" and nobody thought it necessary to install a feedback mechanism. Far too many organisations continue to operate on unchecked assumptions just like this one. Growth and employee turnover provide some people that diligently check, and others that assume common sense prevails. Both employee types *could* make valuable contributions over time (emergence), but a dedicated feedback mechanism *will* continuously prevent waste (predictably).

Completing the feedback Loop

Predicting customer's spending behaviour is like forecasting the weather and predicting the climate. Very short-term forecasts are accurate, but anything beyond a few days has much lower reliability. If the service provided today was valuable there is a high probability the customer will continue to value it next month too. Whether they will value it as much in three years' time is less certain, although they are unlikely to continue paying for it ten years from now.

Resilient organisations manage this situation by coupling their operating system to what is valuable for customers, forming a "closed loop." If demand for a service rises, the feedback mechanism sends a signal to the decision-making process in the form of results. The decision-making system decides how to increase delivery capacity, as we have seen. If demand falls, the decision-making process may place bets to try and stimulate demand, or it may decide to retire a service that is no longer profitable. Just like the thermostat in a household heating system, the decision-making process is the *controller* of the system.

We already saw this feedback loop at the end of chapter 2. Within that loop, we placed a bet on the market and used the results to decide what to do next. In chapter 3, we separated decision-making from delivery, so now the business operates through two interconnected systems. Although they achieve the same overall effect, each system now needs its own feedback loop. The delivery system operates the delivery-monitoring feedback mechanism (arrows 2 and 3), whilst the decision-making system operates the bet-results feedback mechanism (arrows 1 and 4). In Figure 6 below, we see that a bet is the next priority for delivery:

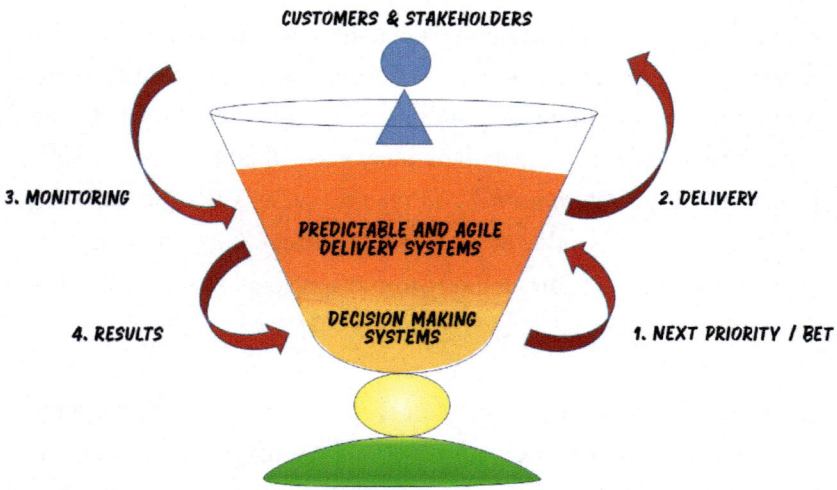

Figure 6 Dual feedback loops of delivery and decision-making systems

The chalice symbolises any department, business area, service, or team you wish to examine. We will look at the pilot for a new method of allocating budgets (wishes do sometimes come true). This is the sequence for feedback:

Arrow 1. The decision-making system (DMS) decides improving budgeting is its next priority and agrees the hypothesis, and how success will be determined, with stakeholders.

Arrow 2. Finance, which is the delivery system (DS) in this scenario, designs and delivers the new method to users and consumers in the form of procedures and training.

Arrow 3 completes the DS loop with Finance supporting the new method in operation by fixing problems and answering questions.

Arrow 4 completes the DMS loop. Decision-makers review the results according to the predetermined success criteria. The DMS then decides what change to make next based on results (did it work as a budget; did it reduce waste) and experience (do people prefer it)?

The DMS's next bet could be reverting to the old method (ending the sequence) or making improvements to the new method and developing a new hypothesis and repeating the cycle again from arrow 1.

In my experience, policymakers and governance-owners fear making changes like this, because the consequences of breaking their organisation's operating system are appalling. And yet, this is an emergent value activity just like launching a new service to the market. With the appropriate controls in place, the risks are manageable. The potential for increasing profits by removing wasteful activities are limited only by the fact that costs cannot be lower than zero.

Powerful Examples

Closing feedback loops can remove costly assumptions and improve performance. These are some recent examples. Feedback loops have:

> Enabled the head of HR to measure the performance of their hiring process. The assumption that hiring was working was closed-off by asking newly hired staff and hiring managers after six and sixty weeks if they felt they were the right fit.

> Showed that telephone-based customer services operators were able to get 100 callers a week to sign-up for web-based access. At that rate, it would take three years to reach the target, so the initiative was abandoned.

> Allowed a senior and long-standing individual to recognise that some of their actions were interpreted as aggressive and counter-productive by colleagues. They accepted an invitation to counselling because they understood the negative impact they were having on others.

Feedback mechanisms and simple controls can help in difficult and uncomfortable situations because they are evidence-based. They provide information without emotion or ego, creating an environment in which people can make better-informed decisions.

Here is an extreme example. TikTok, the app that grossed $177m in 2019[13], was one of hundreds of apps developed using ByteDance's "software factory" approach. For an app-making capability, performance feedback is what really matters:

> *"ByteDance's product strategy is to develop multiple products following a determined strategy and direction, followed by evaluations to see which one works best for more resources. The cost of the trial-and-error procedure is reduced to the lowest considering its mass production capacity."*
> ByteDance: A Chinese Mobile App Factory [14]

Reviewing feedback Mechanisms

Controls and feedback mechanisms are crucial when controlling predictable value activities. They should not be considered "nice to have" options.

Yes, they require human design and human installation, but they will protect their process indefinitely thereafter and help prevent human error. Once feedback mechanisms are in place, continuous improvement becomes possible. It is merely a matter of running one experiment after another. It is hard to think of excuses for not installing them.

Practical Application

I hope I have inspired you to start looking around to notice if controls are in place and feedback loops are closed. As your curiosity for this grows, ask stakeholders if they know about these controls and how they respond to their signals. You may be surprised by what you discover.

5 Amplifying customer Value

This chapter helps you overcome the problems that affect organisations by amplifying customer value and the capabilities that combine to deliver it.

Forces and Amplifiers

The chalice metaphor provides a way for us to visualise and adjust the forces that shape the way work is done in organisations. Managers who are aware of these forces and how they affect what happens at work, organise the local environment to suit the on-going activities. They shape the context, as much as they can, to suit the people involved.

The context is crucial for complex situations, where value emerges from the interaction of stakeholders rather than their physical labour. In such situations, diversity and inclusion are not political statements, but practical ways of increasing the variety and variation needed to understand and address complex opportunities.

In Figure 7 below, I position beliefs and forces in the lower parts of the chalice. Notice how beliefs are an upward force (arrow 1), that shape the context through manager's actions (arrow 2). The performance of the context is measured by its results (arrow 3), which closes the feedback loop by providing new learning for managers (arrow 4):

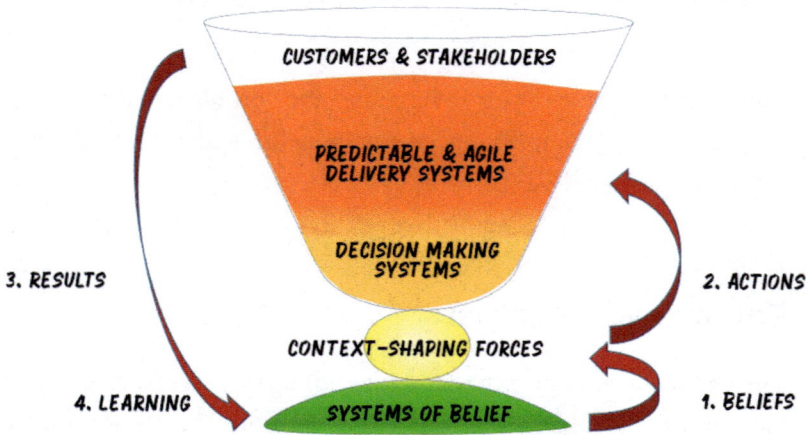

Figure 7 Belief systems add to the environment-shaping forces

It is easy to overlook the importance of the forces in the base and stem of the chalice, just as we may take people's beliefs for granted or barely notice the power in and around organisations.[iv]

Managers' beliefs dominate in organisations. Those beliefs drive managers' behaviours, and that behaviour affects the systems of work. For example, the belief that workers are merely resources, leads to authoritarian style of management, and creates a "command and control" work context. Beliefs, principles, and core values are considered crucial to the leaders of many successful large organisations, including Toyota, Haier, Amazon, and Ray Dalio's Bridgewater. Toyota is interesting because its founders

---

[iv] "Power in and around organisations" is the name of a book by management researcher, Henry Mintzberg.

systematised its management methodology, allowing it to continue using it long after their departure.

Amplifiers and Constraints

Measures of performance, such as employee satisfaction, rates of improvement, and effectiveness of end-to-end value-delivering flows, are all useful measures. By amplifying and making these measures matter, managers change the balance of forces. That is how we create change. For example, if employee satisfaction is being measured for the first time, that measure will change the existing tensions, some behaviours will change, which may affect performance. But nobody can predict *how* it will change behaviour or affect performance. For example:

> If you approach a cheetah. It will probably glance
> at you, then close its eyes, but it may take a swipe
> at you. Your presence will get a reaction, but you
> do not choose what happens.

Amplifiers are one of the most powerful tools in emergent value activities, which is why managers have such an impact in the workplace, often without realising the effect of their actions or words. Managers who have not yet learned to "manage upwards" tend to amplify the demands of their managers. The resulting "I need you to do this because my boss wants it done" is unlikely to be valuable to customers and certainly not motivational.

Imagine how effective you can be as a manager by intentionally amplifying the behaviours you now know are most likely to produce the outcomes you want. The cheetah I stroked was trained:

Animal trainers use positive reinforcement to encourage the behaviours they want repeated. In the case of dangerous animals, they generally ignore all other behaviours.

Incoming Forces

Although I positioned context-shaping forces in the chalice's stem, it is both a concentration of forces and a place from which forces emanate. Physically, it is where the weight of the organisation would meet the equal and opposite force that supports it. I already described management's beliefs as an upwards force, and this is noticeable whenever a new initiative is launched, or a target announced. But what about the forces acting downwards? They are considerable:

Employees feel pressure as it cascades down the hierarchy towards them.

Executives are aware of the expectations of shareholders and stock market analysts.

Compliance officers check policy and regulations are observed.

Managers constantly broker the needs and egos of their peers and stakeholders.

But what happens when one of those forces clash with an individual's fundamental beliefs? Or worse, when a manager is told to do something they believe to be morally wrong or bad for the organisation? It is essential that managers deliver the leadership needed to support people through that crisis and place the present action in the bigger context. Remember, leadership is just one aspect of managing, and leadership is needed at all levels of the organisation.

Healthy Tensions

In an effective work context, tensions are examined and re-negotiated regularly. If the situation above happens more than once, it must be acknowledged and addressed otherwise people will look for work in an environment that is better aligned with their beliefs. Priorities change against strategies, delivery sometimes matters more than quality, and there are times when survival depends on revenue. These tensions always exist, but they need to be balanced. That can only happen if working conditions allow it. Recently:

> The COVID pandemic proved that people could work from anywhere but the tension between enforcing location as a policy and letting people decide for themselves has not been resolved by all employers.

Cause and Effect

It is usually a waste of time looking for cause and effect in complex situations. In an organisation of human activities, no individual, function, or policy is the cause of any observable effect. According to the nursery rhyme:

> Jack fell down as he and Jill went to fetch a pail of water, but did he trip or was he pushed? If he

> tripped, was it on something that was on the path,
> and if so, who left it there?

It is frustrating to be able to see an effect without knowing what caused it. That is because we (mostly) like to know why things happen so we can control them. It is appropriate for complicated and predictable situations, which is why we do root cause analyses, but can be dangerous in complex and emergent situations. In mediaeval Scotland:

> More than 4000 people, 86% of whom were women, were blamed for local misfortunes. They were tried under the Witchcraft Act and at least 2,500 people convicted and executed.[15]

In this case, an act of parliament *amplified* the practice of witchcraft. Not only bringing it to general attention but making it a crime. Whoever suggested keeping cats was evidence of practising witchcraft, would have been ignorant of the cat's effectiveness at reducing the spread of diseases. That discovery would only emerge three hundred years later, when fleas and rats were blamed for the "Black Death."

The moral of this rather dark tale is to be careful what you decide to amplify, whether it be a performance metric or changing a policy.

Capabilities over Silos

One of the consequences of hierarchies is functional silos and managerial layers. These divisions can lead to "them and us" behaviours, with the distance between the business and its supporting functions being particularly wide. In banking, IT staff refer to customer-facing departments as "the business," and are often regarded as if they were suppliers rather than colleagues. People ask for so many changes because it is so easy in this context. When the software developers are on the next floor, or work for your boss's boss, who would not just go and ask for whatever they needed?

The *business capability* lens amplifies customer value instead of internal division. This makes it easier for colleagues to collaborate, and to increase their performance in terms of value delivery. Consider:

> Prioritising new features by developing and testing hypotheses as equal partners in a capability reduces the business' opportunity costs. Owners and users should expect to collaborate fully with technical delivery teams as they develop new products and services. They can complete the feedback loop by working through complexity to clarify outcomes and test assumptions, together.

If putting customer-first and prioritising customer value are such good principles, why do so many organisations do it so badly? Could it be that people at every level of the hierarchy do what their manager tells them to do, rather than what is best for the customer? I am no psychologist, but I suspect self-preservation and fear of consequences play a part. As a manager, you control the physical environment and local context of work, so you must be aware of the barriers they conceal.

Here are some activities that help amplify customer value. They work well in workshop settings and reviews, especially when the most senior manager in the room performs the job of facilitator.

Naming the customer and describing what they Value

Customer value is of the greatest importance to businesses. But not everyone agrees who their customers are, nor what is valuable to them. This causes problems when optimising processes through the value flow because most departments deliver to the next process, not a customer.

Everyone knows the reality, so the problems are usually a matter of naming convention. The stakeholder diagram in Figure 8 below is common in large organisations:

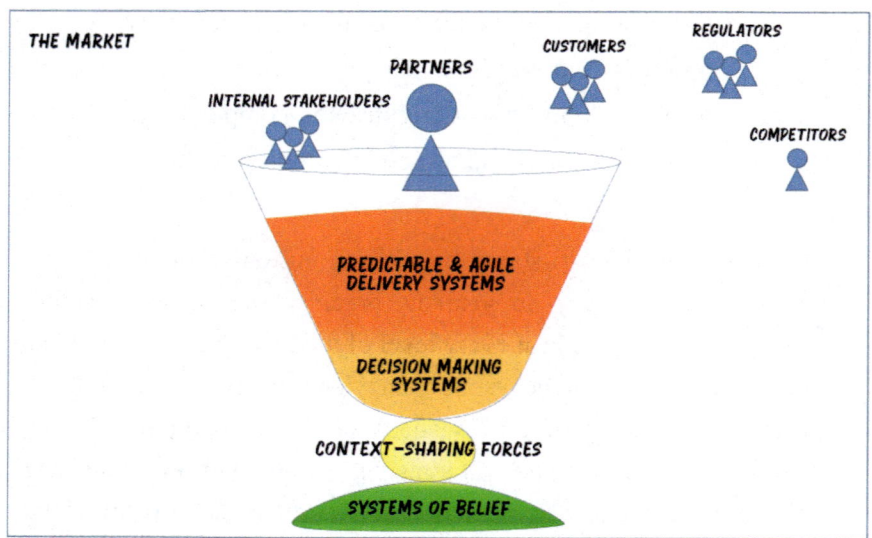

Figure 8 Situation in which supplier has no direct contact with customers

Whereas a small firm has direct access to its customers, most departments of large organisations provide services and products that *enable* customer benefits. They interact with partners, shown in the diagram as partly inside the organisation's boundary, and internal stakeholders such as account managers and "internal customers." Other stakeholders can be represented here too; regulators, competitors, internal audit and risk functions, HR, or legal, depending on the interactions you want to amplify and improve.

Remember, a model helps identify the stakeholders and what each one wants. The facilitator's job is to get everyone involved in a conversation, the output of which may be identification. But the value that emerges from the conversation will be... well, it is unpredictable. In my experience, participants always make valuable discoveries and have powerful insights.

Bringing the customer into the Room

This technique amplifies the partner relationship between any two departments. Often it is IT delivering services to operations, and this approach helps stakeholders move beyond the client-supplier relationship or business-tech gap that often exists. The two chalices represent the separate systems of work, forces, and beliefs of each department.

This is shown in Figure 9 below:

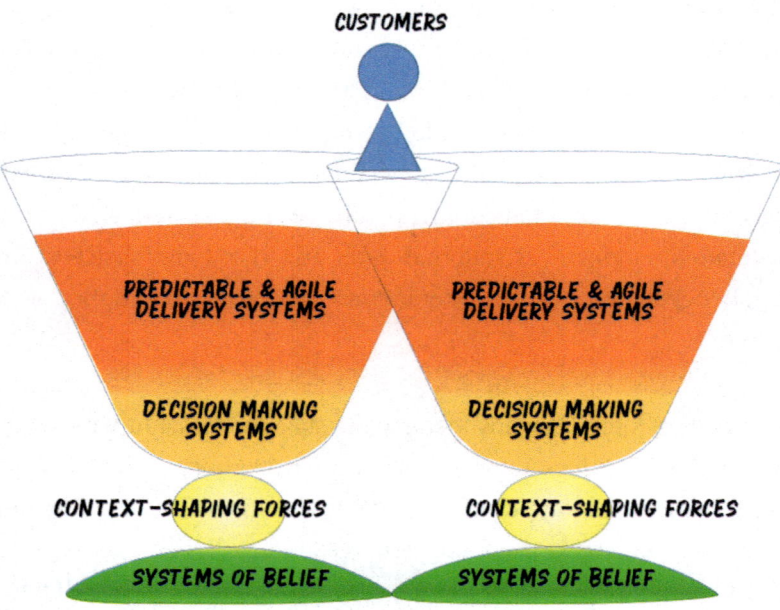

Figure 9 Positioning the customer as the focus between departments

Points to consider when facilitating this include:

> The customer is outside each department but is the shared focus of both.

> Feedback mechanisms and measures must be agreed and created in relation to the customer (eg. bet-results feedback loop from chapter 4).

> Both departments must decide to prioritise the same delivery at the same time, giving it sufficient attention from both sides.

> Both departments experience separate and unique forces and are guided by different belief systems.

Summarising customer Value

What a difference a chapter makes. We went from measurable mechanisms to invisible forces. For those managers unaccustomed to welcoming the whole person into the workplace, with all their weirdness and weaknesses, this may seem unfamiliar. Perhaps a little unsettling. However, it makes sense that the performance of an organisation depends on the healthy relationships of its senior management team. No amount of clever or technical stuff can overcome dysfunctional social behaviours. As Patrick Lencioni says, you need both "smart and healthy" to produce measurable performance.[16]

I developed a couple of ideas from Kurt Lewin, whose research is as relevant today as it was in 1939. His experiment comparing the impact of authoritarian and democratic leadership styles makes for uncomfortable reading when you realise how many of the undesirable behaviours that are normalised in the workplace are the direct result of manager's behaviour.[17]

The use of amplifiers and constraints to effect change in the direction you want it to travel is an adaptation of Lewin's force field analysis. This technique is used to great effect by coaches, as it allows people to recognise which forces are currently driving change and those are restraining it. With this approach, they can see which forces they need to increase and which to dial-down.[18]

Practical Application

I finished this chapter with suggestions for workshop activities in which managers can develop their amplifying and facilitating skills. Unlike predictable value activities, value emerges from complex human systems only if the context allows it to do so. A workshop is a way of stimulating that context, hence my suggestion that you try it. I expect you will achieve better understanding and more effective collaboration, both significant steps towards business agility.

6 Not your grandfather's Workplace

This chapter helps you explore new ways of leading improvement by considering the emerging role of managers.

Reconceptualising the organisation of Work

Pyramids of power and hierarchy have long been embedded into our collective consciousness, but ecosystems and informal networks are emerging as viable alternatives.

One differentiating characteristic of digital age organisations is that their capabilities are dynamic rather than fixed. It is as if they have a capacity for creating and repurposing capabilities, without the need for previous strategy, resourcing, or planning. They simply identify an opportunity that seems worthwhile, develop a hypothesis, deliver it into the market, and measure its performance. For example:

> A friend led a project to create an aerial communications network for one of the tech giants. What surprised her most, was not people skateboarding along the corridors, but that they thought it strange to create a detailed plan before doing the work.

Technology has not only changed the way of work, but it has also changed its markets too. We have seen scarce products being replaced by abundant digital services. Consumers and workers enjoy choices never previously available. Instead of being lucky to get a job in a factory, or hoping to be able to buy a product, people make choices based on on-line reviews and ethical principles.

As the digitalisation of financial, employment, and consumer markets have shifted wealth and power, traditional authority is being challenged. Many of the social injustices that prevailed for hundreds of years are being called out. People are now looking at workplace practices through lenses that expose more than ever before. And, if people disapprove of what they reveal, they use social forces to change it. The digital-savvy generation are as comfortable with complexity as their machine age predecessors are with complication. For instance:

> Social media "influencers" work with the unpredictability of how millions of followers will respond to their words and actions.

> Google started scanning the world's books uncertain of how they would make them available, or if they would ever recover their costs.

> By forbidding the word "exit" at their venture capital firm, the founders of unicorn investor Sequoia Capital knowingly introduced ambiguity into their business.

Some organisations are self-managing (eg. Morningstar, Buurtzorg) others democratic (Semco), distributed, social, or a mixture (Linux). Many are managerless in the sense there are no manager job titles.

No matter configuration or title, there are three "jobs to be done." Leadership is needed to set the direction of change, management to maintain and shape the environment, and action to find a way to the next objective. They cannot be done in isolation because they need contextual information, a variety of skills, and collaboration.

Collaboration to this degree is a surprise when people first experience it. It is not a hand-off from one process to another, nor the delegation of activity down the hierarchy. Those are resource optimisations, freeing one resource by pushing work over the line so it can focus on the next similar task, as in a mass-production environment. In a collaborative environment, people focus on one shared outcome at a time and as a group, often an informal group. When an individual's skills are needed, they step-up and lead. At other times they are present but not observably producing anything.

This evolution is obvious when you realise the flow of customer value is more important than being busy. Busyness produces waste, whilst value flow delivers results. One small delivery is worth more than a million partially developed ideas or works in progress. That is because each delivery yields information about the customer, whilst work in progress is like a traffic jam. Every addition makes it more congested, it will take longer to clear, and the delay means many of those journeys will no longer be worth making. Complexity amplifies these effects dramatically, which is why smart motorways and flight departure boards provide travellers with an estimate of the delay. That tiny piece of information converts a situation of complete uncertainty (an unknown delay) into a situation that is complicated, but which people can resolve themselves.

A pyramid with three layers fails to do justice to any of these ways of working or thinking.

A better symbol for Organisation

My original idea of a cup containing fluid was a better metaphor for the way people behaved within an organisation. The chalice developed over several years, through observation, experiment, and much collaboration. I am indebted to people for their contributions and the conversations that have led to so many insights. Those insights include:

> The chalice is a vessel open to everything around it and describes its own boundaries.

> It describes employees within interdependent systems of delivery and decision-making.

> Its stem helps visualise the forces that concentrate and radiate from there.

> It stands on a base of diverse and inclusive systems of belief that recognise employees are simultaneously within, beyond, and the basis, of all organisations.

No doubt you will find meanings of your own in it. One that really stands-out for me, is this:

> The organisation as a whole has to trust its managers to use their wisdom and humanity to shape the environment of work. Using those forces to amplify either fluidity or rigidity, people or process, emergence, or plans, as appropriate for each activity.

Which leads to the question I was asked in 2015. I remember because it became the subject of my master's research, "what is the role of managers in an agile organisation?"

The role of Managers

Whatever else you are expected to do as a manager, you are obliged to improve the performance of your organisation. Everything you do should support that outcome.

As a manager, you amplify the importance of anything (and everything) you do, point-to, or say. Probably in that order, too. This is a simple consequence of authority and hierarchy. It is how managers wield power, and how managers shape the environment.

Amplifying the 3Cs

Three words, all beginning with the letter "c" are important. They are collaboration, clarity, and competence. As behaviours for managers to amplify, you want to:

> Lead Collaboration

> Ensure Clarity

> Develop Competence

Developing competence has an implied postscript, "…especially your own." Developing your competence as a manager is a leadership behaviour. It is a high-impact behaviour for management because it creates supporting forces that reinforce the other behaviours. If learning is normal behaviour amongst managers at all levels, it will also be a cultural norm. Nobody would need to complain that "we don't have enough time for learning."

The behaviours apply broadly, however they are particularly impactful through the layers of the chalice. Collaboration matters most when stakeholders need to be involved. Clarity when strategies, priorities, and decisions are being cascaded. Competence is one of the factors that inform behaviour, so it is a force that shapes the environment. See Figure 10 below:

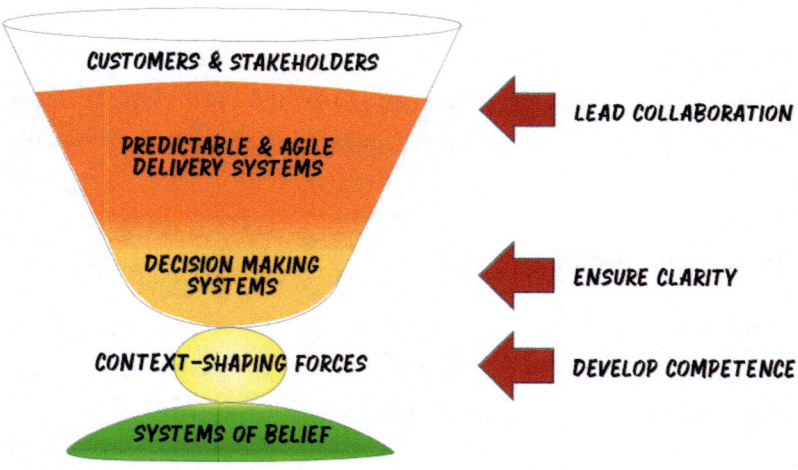

Figure 10 Focus areas for the 3Cs

Leading Collaboration

Customers are outside the organisation and value delivery often comes from the collaboration between two or more stakeholders. We saw in chapter 6, bringing the customer into every conversation amplifies customer value and reduces some of the more distracting forces.

As leaders of collaboration, managers use their understanding of how the organisation works as well as their network of connections to bring the right stakeholders together. Their job then becomes that of facilitator, asking questions from curiosity, such as:

What are the (shared) outcomes we want?

How can we test our assumptions about what is valuable to this customer?

What are the measures that matter in this situation?

What must happen in each of our decision-making systems for us to prioritise this work?

How will we collaborate with the customer, other stakeholders, and each other?

If the forces that shape our environments are not aligned, how can we mitigate this risk?

Notice the manager as facilitator imposes no answers but invites participants to bring their wisdom and creativity into the space created for them. This transfers ownership to the group and helps them to bridge the gaps between their silos. Bringing the customer into focus forms an ecosystem around the customer's needs. This combination shapes the environment for self-organisation, trust, and autonomy. It is how digital age organisations scale and grow so effectively.

The skill to develop is that of supporting others to do the thinking work, without taking over from them. Google's research supports the practice of "manager as coach" being one of the behaviours that differentiates "great managers" from others.[19]

Supporting can be difficult for managers who are used to solving people's problems for them. That behaviour conditions people to wait for their managers to solve their problems. Managers become bottlenecks and the organisation slows-down as decisions line-up to wait for management attention. When managers learn coaching techniques, they become aware of what they have been doing unconsciously for so long. Reflecting on the effect of that behaviour, choosing to change it, and monitoring the outcomes, they are delighted by the results. Not only do they report feeling less stress, but many also enjoy the sense of helping the next generations of managers develop their skills.

Ensuring Clarity

Everyone should know their priorities for work, and it is their manager's responsibility to ensure they have that clarity. This rarely happens because there are as many mixed messages as there are departments, managers, and projects. Ensuring clarity removes the ambiguity caused by conflicting priorities, a problem common in matrix organisations, where employees answer to many masters. Some conflicts come from a single source:

> The CTO (Chief Technology Officer) had commissioned posters that amplified the department's commitment to innovation, quality, and delivery. The inherent conflict was revealed by asking what a developer should do in the last hour before going home, try to invent something, look for bugs, or release the latest changes?

A person's manager may not be the one who prioritises their work, but managers need to ensure prioritisation has happened and been communicated. After that, each team and person are responsible for managing their own work.

Developing Competence

Managers learn their profession by managing and being managed. They adapt according to the context-shaping forces of their places of work and develop through learning and reflective activities. Therefore:

> In an environment where people are valued over processes, managers who support their teams in adapting their processes will be recognised and promoted. They will prioritise learning for themselves and expect it of their staff. The opposite is also true.

Developing competence (especially your own) is a potent context-shaping force that supports learning. By amplifying the fact that managers have more to learn, it normalises learning, making it fashionable or culturally acceptable for others. "If my manager is learning new skills then I want that too." It quashes the absurd notion that managers have special knowledge that makes them solve other people's problems. By leading learning, managers create a self-reinforcing loop through which the organisation continually improves itself.

Knowledge needs to develop at an organisational level as well as individually. If agility mattered to the organisation enough for managers to learn how it works, cooperation, rather than blame would be normal. The typical IT complaint that "we can't get enough engagement from our business colleagues" would seem as strange as their "IT won't deliver what we ask for, when we ask for it" because the gap between the departments would have been bridged. That bridge can be formed by understanding how each depends on the other to support a capability that delivers customer value.

> *"In the long run, the only sustainable source of competitive edge is your organisation's ability to learn faster than its competitors."*
>
> Peter Senge, The Fifth Discipline

If those were not reasons enough to keep developing your own professional competence, consider how much more valuable you will be as an increasingly competent manager. One who has learned how to learn, and how to lead the learning and development of others.

Summarising the role of the manager in the digital Age

I ended this delightfully brief section by challenging the role of managers. The industrial revolution and the evolution of businesses modelled on machines has resulted in a form of management that is not very popular.

My experience, and the evidence-based research suggests that we need to improve the way we organise work, and that depends on the skills of managers. Not by managing people, that is a machine age legacy, but by managing the context; customer value flow, internal tensions, and environment of work.

Table of Figures

References

[1] American Chemical Society. (1999) *The discovery and development of penicillin 1928-1945.* https://www.acs.org/content/acs/en/education/whatischemistry/landmarks/flemingpenicillin.html

[2] Lewis, Russell (2017) *Improving Organisational Agility.* MSc Advanced Computing Staffs University.

[3] Transport for London. (2018) *Contactless payment system update* https://tfl.gov.uk/info-for/media/press-releases/2018/april/half-of-all-tube-and-rail-pay-as-you-go-journeys-across-london-using-contactless

[4] Deming, W. Edwards. (1986) *Out of the crisis.* Cambridge, Mass: Massachusetts Institute of Technology.

[5] Google (2008) *Project Oxygen* https://rework.withgoogle.com/guides/managers-identify-what-makes-a-great-manager/steps/learn-about-googles-manager-research/

[6] Google (2016) *Project Aristotle* https://rework.withgoogle.com/print/guides/5721312655835136/

[7] Cockburn, Alistair. and Highsmith, James. (2001) *Agile software development, the people factor. Computer*, 34(11), pp. 131–133. Available at: https://doi.org/10.1109/2.963450.

[8] Jennings, Ken. (2014) *The Debunker: Did the Model T Ford only come in black?* Woot.com. Available at: https://www.woot.com/blog/post/the-debunker-did-the-model-t-ford-only-come-in-black

[9] Millington, Alison. (2018) *J.K. Rowling's pitch for 'Harry Potter' was rejected 12 times.* Insider.com https://www.insider.com/revealed-jk-rowlings-original-pitch-for-harry-potter-2017-10

[10] Christensen, Clayton. *et al.* (2016) *Know Your Customers' "Jobs to Be Done"*, Harvard Business Review

[11] LitheSpeed. (2021) *Agile Caravanserai Kent Beck.* https://www.youtube.com/watch?v=oXcfwChnfNs

[12] DORA (2021) *Accelerate State of DevOps 2021*. Google Cloud, p. 45. Available at: https://services.google.com/fh/files/misc/state-of-devops-2021.pdf (Accessed: 26 July 2022).

[13] Sensor Tower. 2019. Available from: https://sensortower.com/blog/tiktok-revenue-downloads-2019

[14] China Internet Watch. 2019. *ByteDance: A Chinese Mobile App Factory*. Available from: https://www.chinainternetwatch.com/28055/bytedance-chinese-mobile-app-factory/

[15] *Remembering the Accused Witches of Scotland*. https://raws.scot

[16] Lencioni, Patrick. (2002) *The five dysfunctions of a team: a leadership fable*. San Francisco: Jossey-Bass.

[17] Lewin, Kurt. (1999) *Experiments in Social Space (1939) with commentary by Edgar Schein*, Reflections. Cambridge, Mass. Issue 1(1), pp. 7–13. Available at: https://doi.org/10.1162/152417399570241.

[18] Hardingham, A. and Brearley, M. (2010) *The coach's coach: personal development for personal developers*.

[19] Google (2016) *Project Aristotle* as above.

Printed in Great Britain
by Amazon

31856382R00046